# Leftover Poetry

by

Caleb Delos-Santos

ISBN: 978-81-19228-96-6

First Edition: 2023
Rs. 200/-

Cyberwit.net
HIG 45 Kaushambi Kunj, Kalindipuram
Allahabad - 211011 (U.P.) India
http://www.cyberwit.net
Tel: +(91) 9415091004
E-mail: info@cyberwit.net

# Contents

# Leftover Poetry.

I always eat leftovers.

Unfortunately,
my stomach is contradictory.
Despite my healthily food-filled physique,
my gut endlessly feels empty
and constantly and unconditionally
sucks up everything.

Specifically,
leftover chicken, rice, and sugar cookies
reach and leave my famished lips
within a week of sneaking into my fridge.

Half-eaten pizza,
especially a cheese-stuffed-crust piece with only meat toppings,
sinks through my starving Sarlacc throat
the morning after I order it.

Yet,
my favorite take-home-for-later meal,
my paramount post-purchase calorie snack feed,
my elegant modern manna envy,
is a sausage and pepperoni

*Stromboli.*

After my initial mid-lunch-hour *Stromboli* Mall feast,
this succulent savory leftover beauty
parades through my daydreams.

Each piece of its flimsy liquid cheese
sits in my mind's periphery.

Each steamy seeping pepperoni
gives me the liberating mental pep
I restlessly crave and desperately need
to keep ambitiously reaching artistically.

Each little sausage blip
whips my wailing failing spirit
straight into eternity
and effortlessly breathes into me
unparalleled energy.

No matter what depleting and pointless work productivity
or unexpected yet celestially mapped tragedy
imperfectly plagues me,
all I can see
after copping and chomping on my solid Ichor treat
is *Leftover Stromboli.*

Then, at dinner time,

I finally seize
my grease-lined microwave.

I instinctually thumb-press
my pressure-less 30-second nuke switch.

I climatically reheat
my life-changing Italian blessing.

And, at last,
I triumphantly re-taste
my glorious leftover ecstasy.

*Leftover Stromboli*
deliciously and metaphysically
dominates me
even when I am not hungry.

But,

can *Leftover Poetry*

with back-fridge-forgotten and awfully lost metaphors
or grease-dribbling and in-need-of-rethinking meters
or molding nearly-receptacle-tossed half-ponderings and bad-rhymings

bring me or any stomach
a similarly worthwhile banquet?

*Does Poetry equal Stromboli?*

Or,
are my previously unseen
misfit lines and writings
*freezer-burnt pastries*

with trash heap destinities?

# The Secret Cleaner.

I sit beside a drying mug
with creamless coffee stains
and see a crusting thirsty bug
headbutt leftover veins.

This creature sinks its sable face
into each sticky leak
until this weathered eggshell vase
shines like a baby's cheek.

When done, the cleaner flutters up
to mop another cup.

# Chipmunk.

A fluffy acorn hunter sleeps
on Grandpa's dewed driveway
until she hears my giddy peeps
and rises for her day.

She spots my reaching nut-less palm
and clumsy camera phone
and postures like a dad at prom
or Simba on his throne.

I take one pic with decent grain
and leave this queen's domain.

# Spill.

I siphon soda from a straw
and watch gold bubbles soar
until chilled nectar burns my jaw
and trickles toward the floor.

Brown acid singes popcorn shells
and smashed blue fruit snack goo
until my fizzy spill propels
and hits a stranger's shoe.

I see each flimsy aglet soak
and down my *Diet Coke.*

# Exercise.

A biker wheezes down a hill
beside reclined car seats.
The pedaler's biceps squirm like krill
while drivers nod to beats.

The rider stops to cross the street
and lifts their plastic dome
until a *Tesla* taps concrete
and sends the biker home.

I read about this deadly skim
but still drive to the gym.

# Another Oddity.

While waiting by these crumb-lined stairs,
I eye a wall side crack
that forks like several splitting hairs
and stretches toward a plaque.

This dusty steel cut sheet
wears fading word tattoos
and hangs beside a window seat
that holds three soleless shoes.

I wait and pray to see
another oddity.

# A Poet Hears a Song.

Song and symphony,
Breathing mastery,
Attract my Beauty,
My Literacy.

Metric melody,
Rhythmic harmony,
Charm my Imagery,
My Reality.

Musicality,
Deep vitality,
True humanity,
Spring my Artistry.

# That Hilly Home.

That town-sized house smacked
its bulky yet allegedly expensive
charred-bark-plank skin on stacks
of waned yolk-stained grass.

That hilly home sat alone with nature
or what was left.
Of course, that vacation building's
chalky fume-breeding chimney
sickened it.
It whipped the little blue birds and critters.
It burned the ancient birches with toxic litters.

How could one come to love and defend
that crackling cabin warhead?

Across the eternally glossy cellophane
and strangely copper pipes,
I believe I can see
the cold-souled entity
who calls that overzealous flame shed
their favorite resting homestead.

They carry an anti-weight,
an empty apple crate,
a nature-slaying knife,
a tasteless heightless life.

They crave ecstasy
and hills of luxury.
So, they build relentlessly
and will until they gray everything.
And, if I'm viewing truthfully,

won't we all?

## Horrid Orders for a Plane.

Rise, you plane.
Swarm the sky,
You steel stain.
Make God cry.

Conquer, plane,
You man-spawn.
Become Cain.
Slaughter Dawn.

Why not, plane?
If you can,
Why not drain
Heaven's pan?

Cinder, plane.
Gray each Blue.
Feast, witch-train.
Who'll stop you?

## Long Beach.

Long Beach speaks to me.
Each beaten sky cries softly,
"People are deadly."

# Huh.

Within this sparkly sea of bark and green,
the only creatures I have seen
swim with smoggy death machines.

# Trying to Say Goodbye to a Comet.

I never met you.

I viewed you
as deep dreams fueled your cosmic bursting warmth.
I praised you
and your hug-shaped love-laced spaceflight light.

Then, you died.

I never met you.
But,
I miss you.

# Kid Limb.

While resting in my gray twin bed,
I snatch my sleepless knee
and bring this *Shake Weight* to my head
to burn its energy.

I replicate this twilight crunch
until my leg deflates
and naps from night to early lunch,
where hyper grub awaits.

Once my lips snag a fry or ten,
this kid limb wags again.

## On Beautiful Things.

French Fries,
Tykes' ecstasies,
Clean bruises and "F-streaks."
How could something so healing cause
Cancer?

## Massacre.

I spot a broken soda can
that split from summer heat
and bleeds beside an eggshell van
and one *Starbucks* receipt.

I spy each tire side and find
a splattered *Kool-Aid* pouch
whose venom boils post the grind
and stinks like Elmo's Grouch.

I scope for more car lot "hijinks"
and see more slaughtered drinks.

## First Thoughts.

Illinois is nice.
It's ripe with plateaus of lime.
But,
Does it have a price?

# After Dark.

Why do these steaming clouds retreat
and hide behind an inking sky?
What happenings defeat their might?
Whose actions feed their fright?

# The Thoughts of Hellish Men.

When **Pretty People** loom to me,
my monstrous insides snag my eyes,
drowning them with illustrious lies
and toxic *possibility*.

When **Pretty People** speak to me,
evil feelings siege each reply.
My demons scream as angels cry.
When **Pretty People** flick my skin,
they feed the leeching inner **Sin**
that can consume the sweetest **Guy**.

# How to Internet.

Trickle with Deceit.
Tease. Preach. Ficklely "Retweet."
Bleed. Screech. "Win." Repeat.

## Burning Everything.

Most days, I calmly beam politely
when seeing any local water body.

Yet, on some drizzly weeks,
these slippery little puddles
trip and trickle me.

So, occasionally,
simply defensively,
I poke these lake babies back
with a passive-aggressive
stick of fire.

Once I tap them
with these sparks of sass and wit,
they usually
skittishly flee
like puny sprinkler streams.

Yet, sometimes,
these liquid entities
refuse to leave
and continue to flood me.

In moments like these,
I think they mistakenly believe
they have seen all the fire
inside me.

Regardless,
they will never see
what they are missing

since I can only show
every incinerating intensity
blazing deep within me

by burning everything.

# Growing Old.

Airport rage
comes with age.
Youth blooms *fright*.
Age grooms *might*.

*How dare they!*
Adults say
When helplines
apologize.

*They're the worst!*
Adults curse
and mad hum
with *freedom*.

Adults' *rights*
to flight light
their bloodlust
and disgust.

Adults ream.
Children scream
for release.
*Papa, Please!*

*Mom, don't yell.*
*Don't say "Hell!"*
*Don't hurt me!*
*You're scary!*

Airport rage
comes with age
and frightens
bright children.

## The Many Oo's and You's.

*Achoo!*
**Bless you.**
* * *
*Yoo hoo...*
**Hey, you.**

*You do?*
**I do.**

*¿Y tú?*
**Me too.**

*It's true?*
**Yes, YOU.**

*Yahoo!*
**Woohoo!**

*Love you!*
**Love you!**

*I do.*
**I do.**
* * *
*Hey, you.*
**Screw you.**

*You knew?*
**Mon Dieu!**

*I'm blue!*
**What's new?**

*Screw you.*
**Screw you!**

* * *

*Hey, you...*
**Oh... You...**

*Adieu...*
**Adieu...**

*Wait.*

*Love you...*

You too.

# I Miss My Christian Summer Camp.

I miss my Christian summer camp,
The bunks, the s'mores, the color wars.
I mainly miss *Exhausted Joy*,
Which hit its height on Chapel Night,
When, after days of shakes and screams,
We, kids, could breathe in darkened seats,
And watch some well-lit hippy guy,
Some "once you leave this mountain" guy.
We could unwind, free from the ride,
Free from this life of dying pines,
And tireless times, and *Joyless Strife*.
We could release and sit in peace.

# A Need.

It's strange. I've recently felt more okay.
The change: I've had a string of crazy days
That range from great to awesome. But, they weigh
Estranged on me now since those days won't stay.

Too soon, my age-old boredom will make me
A prune, who needs some action to wake *me*.
Just two unfun days are all it takes me
To skew life's image. Boredom will break me.

But, how can I combat this boredom seed?
What powerful activities can lead
That foul seed to the trash and keep me freed?
For now, I'll write to satisfy my need.

# A Poet's Praise to *Rap*.

I'd like to rhyme
on a dime. But,
each time I try,
rambles fly, and
I cry with spite
for my "whiteness."
My biteless "flows"
can't trade blows with
*true* pros… *Rappers*
*beam blessed burns.* I
puke blurs of slime.
Those *gods rhyme.* I
waste time and whine.

## Decisions.

It's not right that I might not like to write.
I'm a poet. I show it. I owe it
To my own skill to have the will to fill
This page with smarts, with rage, with heart.
Yet, the appeal I feel from sealing words
With pens tends to not mend my fending soul
But pulls wide at its sides. Soon, it might die.
To write might kill me, but to not will still
My drive. To stay alive, I must arrive
At compromise, or is that wise men's lies?
Can one come to some common sum of worth,
Or is Earth worse off that way? Some do say
That sharing is false caring. We're not fit
To split the gold. No. Such old thoughts rot and caught
The past in lasting tension, casting shade
That aided Hell in dwelling over all.
And, despite my whining, I love the stuff I craft.
Each draft frees my eyes to see my mind.
But then again, when the work ends, thoughts lurk.
They say, "Goodbye that day!
You wasted it on tasteless rhymes that'll chime
In no one's mind." These sounds pound me to death.
So, here I fear I lie tied to a pain
Known only to a writer who is stuck
Between two beams of medley deadly art
And life. What fate would the great writer choose?
Who cares? No matter what I choose, I lose.

# The Word.

"Water,"
the word, mirrors
each washing wave and surge.
GOD made WATER, but WHO weathered
"The Word?"

## What a Mess.

I'm One
But Not.

I Act.
I Sing.

I'm One
But Not.

I Write.
I Think.

I'm One
But Not.

I Fight.
I Dream.

I'm One
But Two,
But Three,
But More.

But, If

I
Must Pick,
Which One,

Act
Write
Think
Sing
Fight
Dance
Dream
Tasks
Themes
Cash
Glee
Praise
Age
Peace,

Which One
Is Best
For Me?

# Weigh In.

I step onto my sweat-stained scale
with skinny quaking knees
and pray for water weight to fail
and calories to freeze.

Its blue screen flicks with whites and lines.
My plump heels scrunch and tip
until a code-strung number shines
and rips me like a whip.

This ebony machine shuts down
but leaves me with a frown.

# These Trickling Stairs.

I trickle today
like water
on downtrodden steps:
beginning with weighty
kinetic energy
but
slowly receding,
resigning,
and abiding
by time
until
I dry.

## Slashing Apart an Artsy Tragedy.

Why can't I find my drive for poetry?

Did school erase my creativity?
Did *Canvas* slash my rhyming mastery?
Did group assignments pike my empathy?
Did Spanish tests arrest my ecstasy?

Did college cause an artsy tragedy?
Did I resign my life for some degree?

# "I Am" Poem Assignment - My First Poem

I am alive.

I am a breathing entity.

I am a thinking and feeling personality.

I am a full, functioning living being, with a complex physique, psychology, philosophy, and spirit.

I am a confusing and depressing corruption.

I am a rotting body.

I am dead.

## What is THIS?

Would you call THIS a poem? Would you know?
Do you see my writing lacks metaphor?
Do you sense each line's broken sentence flow?
Can you find my non-working Iambs? Or
Does poor enjambment force you to the floor?
Would you call THIS a poem? Would you swear?
Do crappy rhyming schemes cause you to stare?
Do brainless form-failed poems make you cry?
Can you tell me? Do you even care?
Does THIS mean something? Or, should I even try?

# A Stressor's Chant.

I need to take a bath.
Anxieties have milked my skin.
I need a peaceful path.
My street-beat feet have turned to tin.

I need to freaking breathe.
My stress-pressed screams have cracked my laugh.
I need to freaking leave.
Dear, God. Please, drop me in a bath.

## Bath.

This sacred liquid cakes my skin
with foaming chemicals
that turn my blemished legs to tin
and hairs to tentacles.

I sink below this steaming plane
and drop my stubbled jaw.
Clear nectar tries to find my brain
while I enjoy the spa.

In time, I give each limb a scrub
and leave my little tub.

## A Lazy Chant.

Changes shape my Body.
Changes shape my Soul.
Changes shape my Spirit.
Changes make them Whole.

Resting helps my Wholeness.
Resting helps my Age.
Resting helps my Fullness.
Resting is a Change.

## A Geek's Therapy.

*God Of War*
calms me more
than counseling
or grounding.

*Splitgate* kills
somehow fill
me more than
psalms or Zen.

*Star Wars* fights
soothe my nights.
*Netflix* streams
bless my dreams.

*God Of War*,
techno gore,
and TV
nurture me.

Geeky things rescue me
from my anxiety.
And, is that a bad thing?

# Sculpture.

A purple tree looks down at me
with mighty red eyeholes.
Its metal arms reach crookedly.
I twist my wrists like rolls.

This plated art piece paints my pants
with sun-streamed disco light
while sharpened green-stained leaf-shards dance.
I back away in fright.

Beside this shrine, I read a plaque:
"My Favorite Tree on Crack."

# Fred.

My shower curtain wears a stain
from yesterday's shampoo.
The dark blue ooze flew down the drain
but left clear residue.

This bleach-like outline shimmers more
than each dust-grazed bath screen.
It loosely mirrors King Richard's boar
in shape and milky sheen.

Tomorrow, this blotch might be dead.
But now, I'll name him Fred.

## Does This Fly Believe in Life?

Despite lightning strikes and thunder cries,
this fluffy frazzled Fly
still zooms through windy skies
and tries to find its home before raindrops fly.
Why?

# Response to *Breaking Bad*.

If New Mexico
Is the Sun's favorite plateau,
Why does it still snow?

# Porch Pearl.

What is this reddish orb between
my porch's sunburnt stones?
Did someone drop a metal bean
or friendship bracelet bones?

Does this eroded bead have friends
besides my garden gnome?
What if this pellet makes amends
and prodigally goes home?

What if I cut my probing stride
and bring this pearl inside?

# In Defense of the Unknown.

I don't know why
winged things can fly
or why the sky
muddles sunlight.

I don't know why
wet things can dry
or why neon dye
glimmers at night.

I don't know why
people can lie
or why they die
or why they fight.

I don't know most anything, honestly.
Most people daily live in idiocy.
But, brilliant beings, I must ask plainly,
Why is simplicity a tragedy?

I don't know why those lacking clarity
need to be informed immediately
when knowing everything can't remotely
lead to lasting love or tranquility.

And, shouldn't those simple things
mean leagues more to you or me
than anything worth knowing?

# Contradiction.

The brisk waves bleed gray.
The smudged pier mirrors the display.
What a radiant day.

## I Am an Artist.

My showered ankle levitates
above a gray bath mat
until my blistered big toe trips
and gives its fur a pat.

Steam-twisted bristles tinge to black
and mirror my skin's outline
until my dazzled toe comes back
to paint a faint design.

I brush this fluffy cotton space
and draw a smiley face.

# When I Lose My Mind,

I criticize bright skies.
I snap, rattle, and lie.

I unwind social ties.
I shrink, wrinkle, and fry.

But, when my bride slides by,
my fiery tension dies.

I grind my tired eyes.
I vent, repent, and cry.

## When We Go to Chapel,

She sneezes sweetly.
I bite my felt tip.
She shifts with beauty.
I foot-tap and quip.

I speed-read quiz terms.
She folds paper stars.
I rub touch-screen germs.
She out-sings guitars.

She does her thing. I drift asleep.
We "church" differently.
Yet, when grim feelings creep,

We pray, hug, and love each other
Unconditionally.

# Happy Valentine's Day 2023.

Hey, Love,
Can I tell you why
I like your eyebrows?
Of course, they're tiny, soft, and kind.
But, more importantly,
Those pretty sweet hair-things
Only grow on the one heavenly body
Who undeniably
Means everything to me.

Happy Valentine's Day 2023.

## Token.

My rose gold ring looks back at me
with little glints and grooves
until I twist its steel rims free
to see what it improves.

Without the ring, my skin reflects
a sweaty pasty life
of blisters, cuts, and *Cheeto* specks:
before I found my wife.

I place my circle back with pride
and kiss my shining bride.

# Midnight Peek.

I sink into my purple bed,
compress each fluffy sheet,
extend my sluggish hair-mess head,
and shift my sweaty feet.

In time, I twitch my zit-kissed neck
and twist to my right side
to find a resting heaven speck:
my shining PJ-ed bride.

I look at my amazing wife
and thank God for my life.

# A Poet's Prayer.

Hear me,
Holy King.

Witness me,
Supreme Mystery.

Come to me,
Bringer of Everything.

Free me,
Bleeding Majesty.

Breathe into me,
Exceeding Entity.

Think with me,
Creative Being.

Sing through me
Adoring Glory.

# Make Me

into one
who doesn't Run
from Change,

to someone
who Wonders,
Jumps, and Loves
each Shifting
Day,

even
when
I Age.

www.ingramcontent.com/pod-product-compliance
Lightning Source LLC
Chambersburg PA
CBHW022202160726
48282CB00024B/302
* 9 7 8 8 1 1 9 2 2 8 9 6 6 *